A CULINARY EDUCATION AWAITS
This culinary workbook belongs to Jr. Chef :

_____

© **Copyright 2024**
CHILDREN'S CULINARY INSTITUTE

PUBLISHED BY CHILDREN'S CULINARY INSTITUTE
FOR USE WITH CCI CURRICULUM & BY CCI CERTIFIED INSTRUCTORS
FOR MORE INFORMATION VISIT WWW.CHILDRENSCULINARYINSTITUTE.COM

KITCHEN RULES

Before class

Tie long hair back
Wear uniform apron
Closed toe shoes & short sleeves are best
Read your recipe all the way through
Wash your hands

In class

Follow directions & work with your team
Be cautious in the kitchen & with the tools
No licking fingers or eating while cooking with your team
Wash your hands as often as necessary
Taste the food you make at the end of each class

GOALS

Date

Liquid Measuring

1 GALLON
4 QUARTS
8 PINTS
16 CUPS
128 OUNCES
3.8 LITERS

1 Pint

8 oz. ea.

GALLONS

QUARTS QUARTS

CUPS CUPS
CUPS CUPS
P P
CUPS CUPS
CUPS CUPS

Q Q

QUARTS QUARTS

CUPS CUPS
CUPS CUPS
P P
CUPS CUPS
CUPS CUPS

Q Q

GALLONS

Equivalent

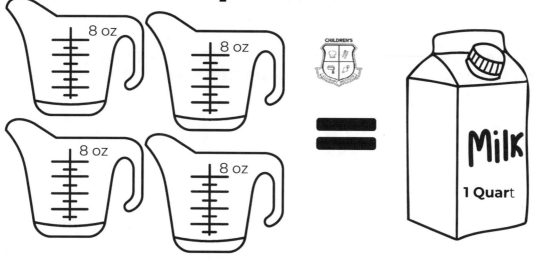

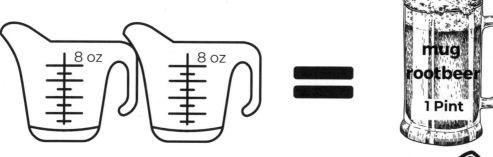

 = **8 oz**

Conversions

°F	°C
250	130
275	140
300	150
350	177
400	200
450	230
500	260

Tastebuds can learn new things

NEW FOODS

Try something new 8-15 times

Don't tell your brain you don't like it before you try it

DATE	New Food	♥ ✓ ⊘	HOW IT WAS PREPARED

Underline the term after you have learned it in class

Glossary of Cooking Terms

Cooking Terms Glossary A

Al dente - The pasta is cooked until tender but still has a firm, chewy texture.

Cooking Terms Glossary B

Bake - To cook in the oven.

Baste - To brush liquids such as fat, meat drippings, marinade, water or juices over meat during roasting to add flavor and to prevent it from drying out.

Batter - A mixture of flour, butter, shortening or oil, and liquid. Batter usually describes cakes, cookies or muffins. A batter is different from dough because dough can be formed into a ball and it keeps its shape.

Beat - To beat means to stir or mix ingredients with a whisk, spoon or a mixer.

Blanch - To blanch food immerse fruit or vegetable in boiling water for a minute or so, remove and place in a bowl of ice water. This is often used before freezing fruits or vegetables. Or you can blanch a fruit or vegetable such as tomatoes or peaches to remove their skins.

Blend - Similar to beat. Add ingredients together and blending them with a spoon or a mixer.

Boil - To cook a liquid such as water or broth so it reaches a boiling temperature. You will see bubbles in the pan.

Braise - To tenderise meat, you brown meat or poultry in oil. Then place in roasting pan and cook in the oven or place directly in the crock pot.

Cooking Terms Glossary B continued

Bread - To bread something is to coat it with bread crumbs, cracker crumbs, or other crumb mixture before cooking it.

Broil - To cook meat or other food under the heat source. This seals in flavor.

Broth - Broth is a liquid made by cooking meat, vegetables or seafood with herbs, bones and water.

Brown - Saute meat or vegetables in a frying pan with oil or butter until it turns brown in color

Brush - To brush food is when you use a pastry brush and brush the top of the food with melted butter or egg white.

Bundt pan - Tube baking pan.

Cooking Terms Glossary C

Caramelize - Browning sugar over medium heat.

Chill - Place in refrigerator.

Chop - To cut food into pieces with a knife, food chopper, blender, or food processor.

Coat -To cover both sides of a food with flour, crumbs or batter. See definition for bread.

Coats a spoon - When stirring liquid in a saucepan the liquid will cover a metal spoon.

Combine -Adding ingredients together and stirring.

Core -To remove the inside of a fruit. Apples or pears are an example of a fruit that is usually cored.

Cream - Mixing butter, shortening or margarine with sugar until smooth and creamy.

Crush - To crush a food into tiny pieces with a rolling pin or kitchen mallet.

Cooking Terms Glossary C continued

Cube - Cutting foods such as vegetables or meat into pieces with 6 equal sides.

Cut in - Blend or cream butter or shortening into a flour mixture.

Cooking Terms Glossary D

Dash - To add a dash of something in cooking is less than 1/16 teaspoon. Since there is no 1/16 teaspoon you use a pinch amount.

Deep Fry - To cook food completely covered in hot oil.

Deglaze - After cooking or roasting meat you add liquid such as milk, broth or water to dissolve the juices stuck to the bottom of the pan. Often deglazing is used when making gravy.

Dice - To cut food into small cubes.

Dilute - To thin a liquid by adding more liquid, usually water or milk, to it.

Direct heat - Direct heat is when food is placed directly on a cooking source such as toasting or grilling.

Dissolve - To dissolve something is to blend food together to make a liquid. For example, add water and sugar together and stirring until sugar is dissolved.

Dot - Add small pieces of ingredients over food for even melting. (usually butter.)

Dough - A dough is a combination of flour, liquid and other ingredients to make a firm mixture usually for bread or cookies.

Dredge - To lightly coat food with flour, bread crumbs or cracker crumbs. See "coat" above.

Drippings - Drippings are what is left in the bottom of a pan after roasting meat.

Cooking Terms Glossary D continued

Drizzle - Pouring a liquid over food in a slow, light trickle.

Dust - To sprinkle food with flour, spices or sugar. For example before kneading bread dust the counter top with flour.

Cooking Terms Glossary E

Egg wash - Blending eggs with water and then coating or brushing baked goods.

Entrée - The main dish.

Cooking Terms Glossary F

Fillet - Remove bones from fish or meat.

Firm ball stage - In regards to making candy. This is when a drop of boiling syrup dropped in cold water forms a ball that will give slightly when squeezed.

Flake - Breaking food apart with a fork usually used for fish.

Flambé - To light a sauce or liquid with flames.

Flute - To press edges of a pie crust together in a decorative way.

Fold - To combine ingredients together carefully by stirring through the mixture and bringing the
spoon back up to the top gently.

Fry - To cook food in hot oil or butter until browned or cooked through.

Cooking Terms Glossary G

Garnish - To add an edible decoration to make food more attractive.

Gel - To let a food set or become solid by adding gelatin.

Glaze - To coat food with a mixture that gives a shiny appearance. For example, a chocolate glaze on a dough nut.

Grate - To shred food into tiny pieces by rubbing against a grater.

Grease - To coat or rub a pan with oil or shortening. For cakes you grease and dust the pan with flour.

Grill - To cook food over direct heat in a grill or direct flame.

Grind - To crush food with a food processor, blender or grinder.

Cooking Terms Glossary H

Hard-ball stage - In regards to candy making, this is when syrup has cooked long enough to form a solid ball in cold water.

Hull - To remove leafs from fruits such as strawberries.

Cooking Terms Glossary I

Ice - To spread a glaze or frosting on a cake or to cool food down by placing on ice.

Cooking Terms Glossary J

Julienne - Cut food into long thin strips.

Cooking Terms Glossary K

Knead - Massage dough with your hands in a back and forth pressing and folding motion for several minutes until dough is smooth.

Cooking Terms Glossary L

Lukewarm - A temperature of about 95°F, not too hot and not too cold.

Cooking Terms Glossary M

Marble - To swirl food together

Marinate - To season food by placing it in a flavorful mixture called a marinade.

Mash - To press food to remove lumps.

Meringue - Egg whites beaten until stiff. Then add sugar to the egg whites. This is used for topping pies or other baked items.

Microwave - To cook food in a microwave.

Mince - To chop in tiny pieces.

Mix - Stirring ingredients together with a spoon or a mixer until well combined.

Moisten - Adding liquid to dry ingredients to make wet but not too wet.

Cooking Terms Glossary P

Pan broil - To cook food in a skillet over high heat by itself and removing fat from pan as it cooks off meat.

Pan fry - To cook with a small amount of oil or butter.

Parboil - To cook food partly in boiling liquid. Also called blanching.

Parchment - Heat-resistant paper used in cooking.

Pare - To peel or trim a food, usually vegetables.

Peaks - Egg whites whipped until stiff peaks form or they stay upright.

Peel - To remove the outer skin of fruit and vegetables with a knife or vegetable peeler.

Pinch - To add less than 1/16 teaspoon. See definition of dash.

Pipe - To use a pastry bag or plastic bag with a corner cut off to decorate food.

Pit - To take out the stone of a fruit such as cherry or peach.

Poach - To simmer in boiling liquid.

Pressure Cooking - To cook using steam trapped under a lid at a high temperature.

Proof - The process of adding yeast to warm water or milk.

Punch down - In regards to baking bread you push down risen yeast dough with your fist.

Purée - To blend food together until it becomes completely smooth.

Cooking Terms Glossary R

Reconstitute - Adding water to dried food to return it back to its original consistency.

Reduce - To boil liquids down to enhance flavor or thicken.

Re-hydrate - To soak or cook dried foods in liquid.

Roast - To cook in an oven uncovered.

Roux - A thickened paste made from butter and flour usually used for thicken sauces.

Rub - A mixture of ground spices that is rubbed over meat and then baked or roasted.

Cooking Terms Glossary S

Scald - To cook just under the boiling point.

Score - Cut diagonal slits on the top of meat.

Sear - To cook meat in a frying pan under high heat to seal in juices. Then the meat is usually cooked in the oven after searing.

Season - To flavor meat with salt, pepper or other seasonings.

Set - Allowing food to become solid.

Shred - To cut with a knife, tear with your hands, or use a grater to cut food into long strips. For meat, two forks can be used to shred cooked roasted meat.

Sift - To remove lumps from dry ingredients with a mesh strainer or flour sifter.

Simmer - To cook over low heat so food or liquid doesn't reach the boiling point.

Skim - To take the top layer of fat from soups or other liquids with a slotted spoon or other utensils.

Cooking Terms Glossary S continued

Skewer - Used for cooking on a stick. Usually wood or metal stick.

Steam - To cook food in a covered pan with a small amount of boiling water.

Steep - To soak dry ingredients in liquid until the flavor is infused into the liquid.

Stew - Cooking meat and vegetables in broth. This works best with less tender cuts of meat.

Stir - To blend ingredients together.

Stir-Fry - Frying cut meat and vegetables on high heat with a small amount of oil.

Strain - To use a colander or strainer to drain liquid off cooked food.

Cooking Terms Glossary T

Thicken - To stir together cornstarch and cold water and then adding to food to change the viscosity

Thin - To add more liquid to food, to loosen the viscosity

Toss - Mix ingredients gently together to combine.

Cooking Terms Glossary U

Unleavened - Baked goods with no baking powder, yeast or baking soda added.

Cooking Terms Glossary W

Water Bath - To cook a dish that is set in a larger pan. The larger pan holds boiling water.

Whip - To beat ingredients together quickly with a spoon or mixer until light and fluffy.

Whisk - To mix together by beating with a whisk or mixer.

Cooking Terms Glossary Z

Zest - To remove the outer part of citrus fruits with a small grater.

Additional terms I learned

....
....
....
....
....
....
....
....
....
....
....
....
....
....
....

OUR KITCHEN BRIGADE

The kitchen brigade system, known as *brigade de cuisine,* is a structured hierarchy that defines the roles and responsibilities of each station within a professional kitchen. This system was pioneered by G. Auguste Escoffier, who implemented it in the kitchen of London's Savoy Hotel in the late 19th century. Even today, it remains a standard in professional kitchens around the globe. We utilize this system in our kitchen to gain insights into the workings of professional kitchens and as a recognition system for our junior chefs!

1) A*boyeur*, is the wait service between the diners & the kitchen. They create smooth operations & unity.

*Serving and working well with others

2) E*scuelerie* is keeper of dishes & keeping the kitchen clean.

*Keeps area clean and helps with clean up jobs willingly

3) *Kitchen Porter* manages inventory, tools & food prep.

*Respects kitchen tools, uses them properly as instructed

4) *Commis Chef* is a novice chef who works under a chef to grow their culinary skills.

*Has an eager learning attitude

OUR KITCHEN BRIGADE

The kitchen brigade system, known as *brigade de cuisine,* is a structured hierarchy that defines the roles and responsibilities of each station within a professional kitchen. This system was pioneered by G. Auguste Escoffier, who implemented it in the kitchen of London's Savoy Hotel in the late 19th century. Even today, it remains a standard in professional kitchens around the globe. We utilize this system in our kitchen to gain insights into the workings of professional kitchens and as a recognition system for our junior chefs!

5) *Entremetier Chef* prepares dishes that do not involve meat or fish, including chopping veg.

*Demonstrates care and basic knife skills

6) *Chef de Tournant* fills in as needed at different stations & positions.

*Sees need in the kitchen and is willing to do the job

7) *Patisier* is skilled in the art of pastries, desserts, breads & other baked goods.

*Demonstrates a creative and quality to culinary efforts

8) *Garde Manger* is a specialty chef in charge of cold food items and storage.

*Keeps a cool attitude and works well in cook teams

OUR KITCHEN BRIGADE

The kitchen brigade system, known as *brigade de cuisine,* is a structured hierarchy that defines the roles and responsibilities of each station within a professional kitchen. This system was pioneered by G. Auguste Escoffier, who implemented it in the kitchen of London's Savoy Hotel in the late 19th century. Even today, it remains a standard in professional kitchens around the globe. We utilize this system in our kitchen to gain insights into the workings of professional kitchens and as a recognition system for our junior chefs!

9) *Grillardin chef* is responsible for any grilled foods.

*Uses caution and safety in the heat of the kitchen.

10) *Fruitier Chef* is a member of the kitchen staff that specialises in fried foods.

*Shows confidence in trying new and challenging skills.

11) *Rotisseur Chef* is in charge of preparing any roasted or braised meats on the menu.

*Takes their time and follows directions completely

12) *Poissonnier Chef* prepares all seafood in the kitchen including stocks and soups.

*Encourages others & gets along "swimmingly"

OUR KITCHEN BRIGADE

The kitchen brigade system, known as *brigade de cuisine*, is a structured hierarchy that defines the roles and responsibilities of each station within a professional kitchen. This system was pioneered by G. Auguste Escoffier, who implemented it in the kitchen of London's Savoy Hotel in the late 19th century. Even today, it remains a standard in professional kitchens around the globe. We utilize this system in our kitchen to gain insights into the workings of professional kitchens and as a recognition system for our junior chefs!

13) *Boucher* prepares all meats & poultry before they are delivered to their respective stations for menu preparation.

*Uses advance knife skills

14) *Saucier* prepares sauces, stews, hot hors d'œuvres, & sautéd foods.

*Shows responsibility by being on time and prepared for class

15) *Chef de Partie* is in charge of any given section and manages the jobs there.

*Most noted for overall good management of their own responsibilities & skills

15) *Sous Chef* is second in command of a kitchen – the one who assists the head chef in all tasks.

*Will be awarded with the opportunity to be the assistant of next session

Children's Culinary Institute
www.childrensculinaryinstitute.com

Chef Recommendation :

These items will support you as you acquire knowledge and skills in your CCI classes, both now and in the future.

- A plastic folder or pocket to organize all your CCI recipes and handouts.
- A CCI tote bag to conveniently carry your apron, workbook, and any other essential kitchen equipment to class.

More books for junior chefs:

Coloring Book for Little Cooks - New Foods
Coloring Book forLittle Cooks - Kitchen Tools
Coloring Book for Little Cooks - Recipes
Write My Own Cookbook - Level 1
Write My Own Cookbook - Level 2
Write My Own Cookbook - Level 3
Food Bridges - The Story of Chef Leah Chase
The Emperor of Chefs - Chef Escoffier
A Pinch of This and a Dash of That - Chef Fannie Farmer
Six Star Chicken - Chef Eugenie Brazier
The Worst Cook in New York - Mary Mallon

By Chef Arlena Strode

Made in the USA
Middletown, DE
16 November 2024

64709670R00015